Warrior Women in Ameri

T0246231

THE ROLE OF
WOMEN
IN THE
GULF
WAR

Warrior Women in American History

THE ROLE OF WOMEN IN THE GULF WAR

Cavendish
Square

New York

Hallie Murray

Published in 2020 by Cavendish Square Publishing, LLC

243 5th Avenue, Suite 136, New York, NY 10016

Copyright © 2020 by Cavendish Square Publishing, LLC

First Edition

Website: cavendishsq.com

This publication represents the opinions and views of the author based on his or her personal experience, knowledge, and research. The information in this book serves as a general guide only. The author and publisher have used their best efforts in preparing this book and disclaim liability rising directly or indirectly from the use and application of this book.

All websites were available and accurate when this book was sent to press.

Cataloging-in-Publication Data
Names: Murray, Hallie.
Title: The role of women in the Gulf War / Hallie Murray.
Description: New York : Cavendish Square Publishing, 2020. | Series: Warrior women in American history | Includes glossary and index.
Identifiers: ISBN 9781502655585 (pbk.) | ISBN 9781502655592 (library bound) | ISBN 9781502655608 (ebook)
Subjects: LCSH: Persian Gulf War, 1991–Juvenile literature. | Women soldiers–United States–Biography–Juvenile literature.Prisoners of war–United States–Biography–Juvenile literature. | Prisoners of war–Iraq–Biography–Juvenile literature. | United States–Armed Forces–Women–Biography–Juvenile literature.
Classification: LCC DS79.74 M87 2020 | DDC 956.7044'2092520973 B–dc23

Printed in China

Portions of this book originally appeared in *American Women of the Gulf War* by Heather Hasan.

Photo Credits: Cover, p. 3 Tom Stoddart Archive/ Hulton Archive/Getty Images; p. 8 Wally McNamee/Corbis Historical/Getty Images; p. 10 William Gentile/Corbis Historical/Getty Images; pp. 14-15, 28, 46-47, 68-69 Bettmann/Getty Images; pp. 16-17 Per-Anders Pettersson/Hulton Archive/Getty Images; pp. 20-21 U.S. Air Force/Getty Images; p. 25 Aviation History Collection/Alamy Stock Photo; pp. 30-31 Getty Images; p. 34 Naval History and Heritage Command/Wikimedia Commons/File:Captain Rosemary Mariner.jpg/Public Domain Mark; pp. 36-37 PJF Military Collection/Alamy Stock Photo; pp. 40-41 Photo 12/Universal Images Group/Getty Images; p. 43 The Advertising Archives/Alamy Stock Photo; p. 50-51, 72-73 Corbis Historical/Getty Images; pp. 54, 75, © AP Images; pp. 56-57 Langevin Jacques/Sygma/Getty Images; p. 59 Jason Meyer/Alamy Stock Photo; pp. 64-65 AB Forces News Collection/Alamy Stock Photo; pp. 66-67 jean-Louis Atlan/Sygma/Getty Images; pp. 78-79 Consolidated News Pictures/Archive Photos/Getty Images; p. 84 Oleg Zabielin/Alamy Stock Photo; pp. 86-87 Llewellyn/Alamy Stock Photo; p. 88 Jessica McGowan/Getty Images.

Contents

Introduction

Throughout American history, women have supported the United States during wartime. But historically their involvement was limited based on outdated ideas about what women are capable of. In the Persian Gulf War, women participated more directly in the war effort than ever before. It was the first major conflict to occur since women had been allowed to enroll in service academies like the United States Military Academy at West Point, and there were more women enlisted in the military than ever before.

The Gulf War began on August 2, 1990, when Saddam Hussein, who became the president and dictator of Iraq in 1979, moved hundreds of Iraqi tanks into the neighboring country of Kuwait. Iraq had been allied with the United States' enemy in the Cold War, the Soviet Union, and there was a history of complicated relations between the United States and Iraq. In the 1980s, Iraq was highly in debt to nearby Saudi Arabia and Kuwait. There was also the issue of land: Iraq's government, led by Hussein, insisted that Kuwait was rightfully Iraqi territory, and furthermore, Iraq claimed Kuwait was producing too much oil and driving prices down.

All of this tension erupted in August when Hussein invaded Kuwait. Though Kuwait was a wealthy country with many oil fields, it was defenseless against Hussein's attack. In less than four hours, the Iraqi army had taken control of Kuwait's capital, Kuwait City, and its oil fields.

The United States and its allies immediately condemned Hussein's actions. Together, Iraq and Kuwait controlled more than 20 percent of the world's oil supply. If Saddam Hussein continued his aggression into Saudi Arabia, as it seemed he might, he would have been in control of nearly half of the world's oil, which could be catastrophic for the global economy.

Thirty-two nations, including the United States, the United Kingdom, France, and Saudi Arabia, joined together to form a coalition against Iraq and Saddam Hussein, led by US president George H. W. Bush. The August of the invasion, President Bush and the United Nations Security Council placed an official ban on trade with Iraq, hoping to cut the nation off economically. On November 29, 1990, the United Nations (UN) told Hussein that if he didn't withdraw the Iraqi military from Kuwait by January 15, 1991, the US-led coalition would take action against Iraq.

In preparation for this, the United States positioned thousands of land, air, and naval forces in the Persian Gulf, an area that includes the countries of Bahrain, Iran, Iraq, Kuwait, Oman, Qatar, Saudi Arabia, and the United Arab Emirates. This concentration of forces in the Gulf region—dubbed Operation Desert Shield by President Bush—was the largest overseas deployment of American troops since the Vietnam War, which the United States was involved in until 1975.

The deadline for Iraq to withdraw from Kuwait passed, and Hussein's troops hadn't left the area. The United

George H. W. Bush served as president of the United States from 1989 to 1993. He passed away in November 2018. His son, George W. Bush, also served as president, from 2001 to 2009.

States responded with decisive action: Operation Desert Shield became Operation Desert Storm in the early hours of January 17, 1991, when the US-led forces launched air attacks on Iraq's capital city, Baghdad, as well as elsewhere in Iraq. Waves of fighter planes bombed key Iraqi military targets such as missile launch sites, heavily fortified command and communications centers, airports and runways, and radar facilities. From that day on, Iraqi forces were under constant, heavy air strikes.

Five weeks of these air attacks nearly decimated Iraq's ability to fight back. Then the ground assault began, as the marine, army, and air forces of the United States and its allies moved into Kuwait, pushing Iraqi soldiers out. The war on the ground lasted just one hundred hours. On February 27, 1991, just six weeks after the beginning of Operation Desert Storm, Kuwait City was liberated.

Of the 540,000 troops who were sent to the Gulf region during Operation Desert Shield/Storm more than 40,000 of them were women, the largest deployment of women to a US military action in history up to that point. The Gulf War also saw expanding roles for women, who served in almost all of the hundreds of support positions that were open to them, including administrators, engineer equipment mechanics, drivers, air traffic controllers, radio operators, and law enforcement specialists.

Although women's roles had expanded in the military, they still weren't allowed to serve on the front lines or in any combat positions. In fact, combat positions wouldn't open to women in the US military until 2013, over two decades after Operation Desert Storm had ended. The support positions available to women were crucial to the

American soldiers arrive in Saudi Arabia in advance of Desert Shield and Desert Storm. The Gulf War was the first major conflict to occur after women were allowed to enroll in US military academies.

war effort, but many women chafed at the fact that they weren't allowed to serve in combat.

The laws preventing women from doing so relied on sexist assumptions about women's ability to fight and the idea that women should be kept out of harm's way, even though women in support positions could wind up in just as much danger as the men on the ground, as Iraqi long-range missiles targeted staging and supply areas as well as the front lines. During the Gulf War, women were shot at, wounded, captured, and killed. They were also decorated for valor.

The women who served in the military during the Gulf War joined the military for many different reasons, but they were all working for a common cause. Despite limitations on the roles they were able to take, they showed that women are as capable as anyone at making a difference in a war effort. Their bravery, loyalty, and dedication to their fellow soldiers and their country is admirable, and the stories that follow attempt to honor their work.

Women of the Air Force

Women have participated in the Air Force since it was established as a separate branch of the United States military in 1947, and they have officially been able to enlist since July 1948. But the roles female Air Force members were allowed to take on were far more limited than those available to men. Women began flying for the military in World War II, helping ferry supplies and planes to key sites with the Women Airforce Service Pilots.

In the early 1950s, during the Korean War, most women in the Air Force continued to work in support roles behind the scenes and were only allowed into combat zones as nurses on medical evacuation flights. Women were finally able to become generals in the Air Force in the Vietnam War, and in 1973 a landmark Supreme Court case called *Frontiero v. Richardson* led to the dissolution of the Women in the Air Force program, allowing women to enlist as Air Force service members equal to men.

By the time the Gulf War began, women were able to serve as pilots and copilots on refueling missions and other service flights. Approximately 5,300 Air Force women were deployed for the Persian Gulf War in various positions. Though they couldn't serve in combat positions (and wouldn't be able to until 1993, after the Gulf War), the women who served with the Air Force played a pivotal role in the outcome of the war.

Hours in the Air

Lisa Stein was born on March 9, 1965, in White Plains, New York. She decided to join the military because she "thought it sounded like fun and they would foot the bill for school."[1] To this end, she obtained a four-year Air Force Reserve Officer Training Corps scholarship to the University of Miami, Florida. Upon her graduation in 1987, Stein was commissioned into the United States Air Force. Following her basic training, Stein was assigned to an Airborne Warning and Control Systems (AWACS) unit. She accrued more than 1,800 hours of combat flight time, despite rules restricting women from flying combat missions, before being deployed to Saudi Arabia in 1990 for Operation Desert Shield.

During Operation Desert Storm, she served as a navigator on board the AWACS. These planes, equipped with large, rotating radar discs, were used for surveillance during the war. Designed to oversee all aircraft in their operating area, AWACS identified planes as either friend or foe and then dispatched an appropriate response to deal with threats. During Operation Desert Storm, the air traffic control that was provided by AWACS, such as the one in which Lisa Stein flew, prevented catastrophic midair collisions by allied aircraft. From January 17, 1991, to March 1991, serving in such a manner, Stein accrued more than six hundred combat flight hours.

The Women Airforce Service Pilots (WASP) was an organization of female aviators who trained as test pilots, ferried aircraft from factories to bases, and trained other military pilots during World War II.

The Burning of Kuwait

During Operation Desert Storm, Iraqi troops set fire to over six hundred oil wells located in Kuwait. Saddam Hussein had promised that "if he had to be evicted from Kuwait by force, then Kuwait would be burned," and that's exactly what happened as Iraqi troops were evacuating Kuwait.[2] It was estimated that about 5 million gallons (19 million liters) of oil were going up in flames each day. When the war ended, 650 oil wells were still burning, and the last fire was not put out until November 1991.

The burning of the oil fields caused immense amounts of smoke and oil rain to fill the desert air. Still winds then caused the plumes of smoke to drop down to the ground, where the troops were. At times, the smoke was so thick that troops were only able to see about

Firefighters haul water hoses as a Kuwaiti oil field burns in the background on August 14, 1991. In February 1991, specialized firefighters were sent to attempt to extinguish the burning oil field.

10 feet (3 meters) in front of them. Since the Gulf War, many veterans have complained of symptoms such as shortness of breath, headaches, and memory loss. Some believe that these symptoms can be linked to the smoke and petroleum that they were exposed to while in the Gulf.

These fires buried much of the Persian Gulf in a poisonous smoke. Exposure to such oil fumes damaged Stein's eyes and led to a loss of her peripheral vision. As a result of this disability, she retired from the Air Force, having achieved the rank of captain, in September 1992. During her military career, Stein received such decorations as the Air Medal with BOLC (Bronze Oak Leaf Cluster— this indicates that more than one of the awards it was listed with was received), the Aerial Achievement Medal, the Air Force Outstanding Unit Award with BOLC, the Combat Readiness Medal, the National Defense Service Medal, and the Air Force Overseas Short Tour Ribbon.

"Flying Nerve Centers"

Captain Sheila Chewning also served on one of the Air Force's AWACS during the Persian Gulf War. Due to the vital role that AWACS aircraft played in the air campaign, they were often referred to as the "flying nerve centers" of Operation Desert Storm. Communication was key to the success of the air campaign. With more than two thousand airplanes coming and going around the clock, it was important that everyone be coordinated. AWACS made that possible. Not only did they control air traffic in the area, keeping coalition aircraft from crashing into each other, but they also spotted enemy planes and led allied aircraft to them. According to an article in *Air Force*

Key Support Roles

Although they were kept from directly serving in combat missions, women flew aboard tanker aircraft, which carried out the task of refueling bomber and fighter planes; aboard transport aircraft; and on Airborne Warning and Control Systems (AWACS) aircraft, which helped control air traffic. Women also served at air bases, where they serviced, repaired, and armed the aircraft that were headed for combat. Though not technically combat positions, these jobs could be very dangerous. The support aircraft and air bases were frequent targets for enemy missiles. Despite the risks, the roles that the Air Force women played during the Persian Gulf War helped the Air Force to attain its goals of striking enemy targets in Kuwait and Iraq, transporting Army and Marine forces by air into strategic positions, and providing air support for the ground troops.

Magazine, AWACS "played a major role in all but two of the coalition's 40 air-to-air kills of the Gulf War."[3]

As a weapons controller, Chewning utilized the sophisticated radar equipment on board the AWACS to direct US fighter planes into strategic positions relative to enemy aircraft. During one of the first dogfights (aerial battles) of the war, she aided in shooting down two Iraqi fighter planes.

Also, during the first bombing raid on Baghdad, Captain Chewning orchestrated the downing of two Russian-built Iraqi MiG-29s by US F-15 fighters. It was a tense moment. After directing the US fighters in the attack, Chewning anxiously listened to her radio as the fighter

The F-15 Eagle is a type of fighter aircraft that has been in use since 1976, though as of 2019, production of the aircraft was scheduled to end in 2022. It was designed for use in all kinds of weather.

pilots located the MiGs, fired upon them, and finally announced that they had shot the enemy aircraft down. "The minutes between hearing the pilots say 'contact,' 'engaged,' and then 'splashed' seemed like a long, long time," Chewning recalled.[4] However, it was times like these for which she was trained. "When that happened [bringing down an enemy plane], we really felt like we were doing our jobs."[5]

On the Ground, Behind the Scenes

Maintenance was another vital role, as keeping planes in good condition and ready to go was crucial to their successful deployment. During the Persian Gulf War, Air Force staff sergeant Laura Long, of Sandusky, Ohio, served as a vehicle operator-dispatcher with the First Tactical Fighter Wing. Her job included making sure that the vehicles were maintained, accounting for the vehicle fleet, and organizing and directing vehicle transportation in support of missions.

Long did say that if there had been an opportunity for her to do so, she would have liked to have been a combat pilot. However, due to the federal law at that time, which prohibited Air Force women from serving in direct combat roles, she resigned herself to the fact that she would just have to take what she could get.

As a supervisor during the war, Long felt that she should be there for everyone. During frightening Scud missile alerts, she worried about her drivers, wondering if they were all OK. Even though a missile could have ripped through the building in which she worked at any moment, Long, who was dressed in a chemical suit and a gas mask, bravely stayed in her office making calls to her drivers instead of taking shelter in the bunkers with the rest of her colleagues.

Working Together

That sense of community and caring for one another was a key part of Air Force sergeant Sherry Callahan's experience of serving in the Persian Gulf. Of her service experience, Callahan said, "I learned a lot during the war, but the point that sticks with me the most is that whenever it got tough, everyone rushed to help."[6]

Callahan was an assistant maintenance crew chief with the First Tactical Fighter Wing during the Persian Gulf War. She served as a shift boss in charge of maintaining an F-15 fighter plane that she affectionately called Daphne. "We do practically everything," she stated. "We wash it. We do maintenance on it. We take care of it, just like a personal car. Except that we can't take it home."[7]

Callahan's unit reached Saudi Arabia on the second day of Operation Desert Shield, having made a long fourteen-hour flight. After arriving in the Gulf, Callahan labored to keep Daphne in working order. She took pride in her work, and it showed. She boasted, "It [the F-15 fighter] hasn't broken since we got here."[8]

As the boss of the team that maintained the F-15 fighter, Callahan was not only responsible for the condition of the aircraft but also the safety of the pilot who flew the plane, Colonel John McBroom. A malfunctioning plane could mean disaster for its pilot. Without Callahan, Colonel McBroom, commander of the First Tactical Fighter Wing, would not have been able to carry out his duty. During Desert Storm, the F-15 fighters who operated mainly at night in order to hunt Scud missile launchers and artillery sites were key to Air Force victories during the war.

The No-Nonsense NASA Alum

Born May 22, 1953, Stephanie Wells became interested in aviation while in high school. Her role models were such heroines as Jacqueline Cochran and Amelia Earhart, both female pilots. Following high school, Wells entered Iowa State University, and upon the completion of a degree in meteorology in 1975, she became the first woman to graduate from the school's Reserve Officers Training Corps (ROTC) program.

Wells entered active duty with the Air Force as a weather officer. After ten years, she joined the reserves, serving part-time as a C-5 aircraft commander and full-time as a National Aeronautics and Space Administration (NASA) staff pilot. It was at this time that tension was escalating in the Gulf. Within days of President Bush's August 6, 1990, announcement that troops would be sent to Saudi Arabia for Operation Desert Shield, Wells was flying worldwide C-5 missions while continuing her work as a NASA staff instructor pilot. By August 29, 1990, Wells's reserve unit, the Sixty-Eighth Military Airlift Squadron of the Military Airlift Command, was called to active duty, becoming part of the largest airlift operation in military history.

When Operation Desert Shield became Operation Desert Storm in January 1991, Wells wrote in her diary, "The attack has begun at long last."[9] Up to this point, Wells had nervously anticipated the start of the war, but with the attack, her attitude changed to one of "Go get 'em and get this thing over with."[10] To her, the anxiety

Jacqueline "Jackie" Cochran is best known for her role in the formation of the Women Airforce Service Pilots during World War II. She was also the first woman to break the sound barrier.

of waiting for the war to begin was much worse than actually being in it. During Operation Desert Storm, Wells amassed six hundred hours of flying time, transporting cargo to and from the desert. This cargo included tanks, trucks, helicopters, missiles, medical supplies, food, and some troops. She made twenty-two flights into dangerous hot spots such as Saudi Arabia, the United Arab Emirates, and Egypt.

Many of her missions were also quite long, averaging fourteen days. Wells retired from the reserves in 1996 as a lieutenant colonel, having served twenty-one years in the military. Few military pilots could match Wells's combined experience in the Air Force and in NASA.

Women of the Navy

Women began working unofficially with the United States Navy during the American Civil War, and officially beginning with the establishment of the United States Navy Nurse Corps in 1908. At first, only twenty women were selected for the program. These women, the first to serve officially with the US Navy, became known as the "Sacred Twenty," though the group eventually expanded to over 150 members by the time World War I began. The personnel demands of World War I led military officials to open enlistment to women, who would serve in administrative positions throughout the force, and in 1917, Loretta Perfectus Walsh became the first female sailor in the Navy.

In the 1970s, for the first time women were allowed to work on ships, as long as they weren't in combat, and in 1972 Alene Duerk became the first female admiral. Women were finally allowed to participate in naval aviation training beginning in 1973, and by the end of the decade were involved in nearly all naval operations except for direct combat. During the Gulf War, the primary responsibilities of the Navy, beyond participating in the attack, were stopping Iraqi trade and providing protection to American and allied ships. Navy vessels also provided most of the supplies to American military forces, including

Loretta Walsh was the first woman to join a branch of the US military as something other than a nurse. Walsh is pictured here on March 21, 1917, the day she was sworn in as a chief yeoman.

ammunition, weapons, and even planes. They also transported troops. When it came to the attack, Navy ships fired missiles on Baghdad and Kuwait, opening the way for allied ground forces during the ground war. The first shot fired in Operation Desert Storm was, in fact, fired from a Navy ship.

Approximately 3,700 Navy women were deployed for the Persian Gulf War. Though women were kept from serving on combat ships, they played a crucial role in the contribution that the Navy made to the war. Women served on hospital ships, providing medical care to thousands of military personnel. They also served aboard ships that provided ammunition, repair, and essential supplies

Noncombatants

During the Gulf War, Navy women technically participated in combat, either directly or indirectly, though women were not allowed to serve in combat until 2013, when the ban on women in combat was finally lifted. In 2016, all combat jobs were officially made open to women and individuals assigned female at birth in general. But during the Gulf War, none of these options were available: the women of the US military were only allowed to take noncombat positions. While many of these "behind the scenes" roles were just as important as combat positions, the restrictions on women did influence the kind of impact they had in the Gulf War, though not their significance, or even the danger involved. The support vessels on which the US Navy women sailed were not out of harm's way. These ships often went without the protection of the fleet and were vulnerable to missiles and floating mines.

to the entire American fleet. Women also served ashore in fleet hospitals, in construction battalions, and in several other support positions.

Comfort and Mercy

In 1968, Bonnie Burnham Potter earned her bachelor's degree in animal science from the University of California at Davis. She later went on to receive a doctor of medicine degree from the St. Louis University School of Medicine in 1975. Potter completed her internship and residency in internal medicine at the Naval Regional Medical Center in Oakland, California. She worked at the Naval Regional Medical Center as chief resident from 1978 to 1979 and then continued there as a staff internist and residency training officer until 1983.

In August 1990, Potter was deployed in support of Operations Desert Shield and Desert Storm, and she remained in the region until April 1991. She served on

Potter served as a nurse on the USNS *Comfort*, the hospital ship pictured here. The red cross symbol marks medical support vehicles and vessels throughout the armed forces.

board the USNS *Comfort*, a naval hospital ship, as head of medical services.

The USNS *Comfort* was called up for duty in support of Operation Desert Shield on August 9, 1990. On August 11, the hospital ship departed from its home port in Baltimore and sailed toward the Persian Gulf, arriving on September 8. During Operation Desert Storm, the *Comfort* was positioned very close to Kuwait, just off the coast of Saudi Arabia. The *Comfort* shared these waters with the only other US Navy hospital ship, the USNS *Mercy*. During its eight-month deployment, the *Comfort* traveled more than 35,000 miles (56,327 km), consuming nearly 3 million gallons (11.3 million L) of fuel. While in the Gulf, the staff on board this hospital ship saw more than eight thousand outpatients and performed 337 surgical procedures.

This thousand-bed hospital ship was equipped with operating rooms, intensive care units, and advanced diagnostic equipment. The medical staff on board the ship were prepared, if it had been necessary, to treat servicemen injured by chemical and biological weapons.

Following the Persian Gulf War, Potter continued her service in the United States Navy. She served in such positions as commander at the National Naval Medical Center in Bethesda, Maryland; as chief of the medical corps at the Bureau of Medicine and Surgery in Washington, DC; and as fleet surgeon for the US Atlantic Fleet. Potter was promoted to rear admiral in 1997 and received her second admiral star in 2000.

Rear Admiral Potter's military decorations include the Defense Meritorious Service Medal, the Meritorious Medal with gold star, the Defense Superior Service Medal, the

Legion of Merit with gold star, the Navy Achievement Medal, the Navy Commendation Medal, the Combat Action Ribbon, and several other campaign awards.

Naval Jet Planes

Though the Navy makes most people think of ships and submarines, it also has a large aviation program, as planes can play a key role in naval warfare. Launched from the decks of barges, naval planes can be used for medical and other support missions, as well as for attacks. Rosemary Bryant Mariner was one of the first women to become a United States naval aviator.

Born on April 2, 1953, in Harlingen, Texas, Mariner joined the Navy in 1973, becoming one of the first eight women to enter military pilot training. In 1974, Mariner became the first woman to fly a tactical jet aircraft when she piloted the A-4E/L Skyhawk, a jet-powered light-attack bomber. She made history again, just a year later, when she became the first female pilot to fly in a frontline combat aircraft, the A-7E Corsair II.

One of the major concerns that the Navy's battle groups faced throughout the Persian Gulf War was antiship missiles from Iran and Iraq. During Operation Desert Storm, Mariner commanded an electronic warfare squadron. Electronic warfare is military action that utilizes electromagnetic energy to obstruct, damage, or destroy an enemy's electronic equipment. It also involves warfare that uses electromagnetic energy as the destructive mechanism of weapons, such as laser beams. Electronic warfare also serves to immediately recognize and provide protection against an enemy's use of such energy.

Captain Rosemary Mariner wears her official naval uniform, including the winged pin worn by naval aviators. Mariner was the first woman to serve as commander of a naval aviation squadron.

Mariner's squadron, Tactical Electronic Warfare Squadron Thirty-Four, was a training squadron that served to prepare battle groups to respond to antiship missiles. During training exercises, Mariner's squadron played an adversary role, acting as the enemy against coalition forces. By utilizing the equipment and tactics in the same way that a potential enemy would, Mariner's squadron helped to prepare allied forces for an actual attack. This was an important job, because it gave the battle groups the skills and confidence that they needed in order to handle real-life situations.

In 1997, Mariner retired from the Navy as a captain, having served twenty-four years as a naval aviator. During her time in the military, she logged more than 3,500 flight hours in fifteen different types of naval aircraft and made seventeen landings on aircraft carriers. Mariner worked at the Center for the Study of War and Society at the University of Tennessee in Knoxville from 2002 to 2016. In 2019, she sadly passed away from cancer.

Flying the Sea Knight

Planes aren't the only flying vehicles used by the Navy. Thanks to their unique ability to hover in place and land nearly anywhere, helicopters can be especially useful in rescue missions and for ferrying supplies. Naval helicopter pilot Brenda Holdener was born on November 28, 1960, in East Saint Louis, Illinois. While in high school, she decided to join the Navy. Following her 1978 high school graduation, Holdener received a Naval Reserve Officers Training Corps (NROTC) scholarship to a state university. She graduated from the university with a degree in construction engineering management and

In this August 2011 image, Captain Brenda Holdener, commanding officer of the USS *Wasp*, gives instructions to her crew as they prepare to leave Virginia in advance of the approaching Hurricane Irene.

was commissioned into the United States Navy in June 1985.

Holdener served for two years as a general unrestricted line officer, assigned to the Naval Manpower Engineering Center in San Diego, before being selected for the naval aviation program. She received her wings in July 1988 and was detailed to fly the H-46 Sea Knight, a helicopter used for such purposes as moving troops and equipment, medical evacuation, firefighting, heavy construction, and search and rescue.

Holdener served briefly in Norfolk, Virginia, before being deployed to Saudi Arabia for the Persian Gulf War. During the war, she served as Detachment Seven officer in charge aboard the USNS *Sirius* (T-AFS 8). The *Sirius* is a combat stores ship that delivers goods to combat ships with the help of the two H-46 Sea Knight helicopters that are assigned to it. As one of the pilots of these helicopters,

Holdener carried out the important task of ferrying essential supplies such as fresh food, clothing, repair parts, and mail to US ships on the Red Sea during the Persian Gulf War.

The H-46 Sea Knight helicopters, like the ones in which Holdener flew, have served the Navy and Marine Corps in all combat and peacetime environments. These aircraft fly day and night in any weather, faithfully supplying operations that take place on the water and on land. On being a woman in the Navy, Holdener stated, "We're not without the guys who don't want us there, but that just makes women work harder and want to be there."[1]

Holdener's personal decorations include the Meritorious Service Medal, a Navy Achievement Medal with one gold star, a Navy Commendation Medal with two gold stars, and several unit and operational awards.

The Dangers of Chemical and Biological Warfare

Petty Officer Sandra Hormiga was born on November 21, 1964, in Houston, Texas. Hormiga, who served in the United States Navy from August 1987 to August 1991, was one of many Hispanic women in the Navy who were deployed overseas during Operation Desert Shield/Storm. During the war, she served aboard the ship USS *McKee*, a submarine tender that provided support to submarines and surface combatants. Hormiga, along with the rest of the crew of the USS *McKee*, served to provide everything that a submarine might need, from repair materials to medical supplies.

Throughout the Gulf War, there were serious concerns that Saddam Hussein would use chemical or biological weapons on coalition forces. Chemical and biological weapons are weapons of mass destruction, which are, by definition, capable of easily killing thousands of people. Any manufactured chemical that is used to kill people is considered a chemical weapon. Biological weapons use viruses, bacteria, or toxins that come from bacteria. The first chemical weapons were used in World War I.

Following this, it was decided that those weapons whose effects cannot be predicted or controlled were too dangerous. A treaty, called the Geneva Protocol, was put into place in 1925. Since then, it has been signed by most of the nations of the world. However, the protocol has several loopholes, including the fact that it does not prohibit the manufacture of or the threat to use these weapons. It also does not mention punishment for violators of the protocol.

During the Gulf War, the United States military feared the use of Iraqi chemical and biological weapons because it was known that Iraq had done extensive research on these topics. The most likely way that chemical or biological weapons would be used on the battlefield would be through distribution by exploding bombs or missiles. During the Gulf War, US military personnel wore gas masks and completely covered their skin when such attacks were deemed possible.

In preparation for such attacks, protective masks and clothing were issued to the troops. Medical personnel were also trained in the decontamination and treatment of potential victims. As the USS McKee made its way to the Middle East, its crew, including Hormiga, performed many drills in preparation of possible chemical attacks. One day, while performing a general quarters drill, it suddenly

Members of the League of Nations pose at the 1925 Geneva Conference, where the Geneva Protocol, which prohibits the use of unpredictable biological and chemical weapons, was signed.

dawned on Hormiga that one of these drills could turn out to be real. She realized, "We were no longer 'just doing drills,' we were practicing saving our own lives."[2] From then on, Hormiga treated each drill as if it were an actual chemical attack. Though allied forces were prepared, they were not faced with any chemical or biological attacks.

Women on the Ground with the Army

Women have served in the US Army in some capacity for the entirety of United States history, primarily as nurses, though occasionally as soldiers while disguised as men. The first women to serve with the Army not as nurses were the members of the Women's Army Corps (WAC), established during World War II so that women could be recruited to work in a number of behind-the-scenes capacities, including as switchboard operators and mechanics. These positions had previously been held by men, but all able-bodied men were needed to fight on the front lines in Europe, so women were recruited to fill in. The WAC was officially disbanded in 1978, and men and women transitioned into working alongside each other in various specialties. By the time the Gulf War began, women were allowed to work in any noncombat position in the Army.

During the Gulf War, the task of the Army and Marine forces was to defend Saudi Arabia from invasion and to push the Iraqi army out of Kuwait. When the ground campaign began in the early hours of February 24, 1991, most of the Iraqi troops fled at the mere sight of the US ground troops. Those that did not were either captured

Posters like this one from the 1940s encouraged women to support the war effort by enrolling in the WAC. WAC members worked in any number of jobs, including as mechanics and translators.

or killed. The ground war lasted for only one hundred hours, or four days, and with its end came the end of the Persian Gulf War.

Shifting Definitions of Combat

Of all the women deployed in the Gulf War, the number of those in the Army—approximately twenty-six thousand—far exceeded the other branches of the military. Women served in important roles, such as tank mechanics, keeping the tanks in working order; truck drivers, hauling important equipment and fuel to frontline units; and guards, protecting bases from terrorist attacks and watching prisoners of war.

The Army differed from the other branches of the military in that, while the Air Force, Navy, and Marines had a federal law prohibiting women from serving in direct combat roles, the Army only had internal policies, which paralleled those laws. These policies forbade women from serving in the front lines and in units that participated in direct combat. However, due to the sophistication of the weaponry used during the Gulf War, it was not often clear where the front line was. Long-range Iraqi artillery could easily reach women who were serving in noncombat units or in units in the rear. Noncombat units were fired upon and often had casualties. Support positions in which the women served also often took them into the thick of the battle as they followed the forward units that they were supporting.

Danger "Behind" the Front Lines

Carol Barkalow was born on December 26, 1958, in Neptune, New Jersey. Barkalow planned to join the military after graduating from her upstate New York high school.

As her graduation neared, Barkalow was convinced to attend West Point by a guidance counselor who stopped her as she cut through the school's guidance office. At the time, she did not even know where West Point was, but the guidance counselor informed her that they were accepting women, so she applied. Barkalow was admitted, and on July 7, 1976, at age seventeen, she entered the first class at West Point to include women.

At West Point, Barkalow and her classmates experienced grueling physical training and merciless hazing practices. However, these experiences only increased her determination to succeed.

After graduating from West Point, Barkalow worked for a while in air defense in Germany but found that there were few positions open to women. Barkalow decided to switch to a career in transportation, and when the Persian Gulf War began, she volunteered as a transportation specialist. During the war, she served as a combat support officer, commanding a truck company that used light- and medium-weight vehicles. There were more than seventy vehicles and 140 soldiers.

Of the men in her unit, Barkalow said: "There was hesitation on their part, not knowing what to expect. But it didn't take them long to discover that I was committed to taking care of them. After they saw that, they didn't have a problem. The overriding factor is professionalism."[1] As part of a support unit, Barkalow's company provided assistance for the lead combat brigade in the 24th Infantry Division.

In the early hours of the war, Barkalow's unit moved into Iraq with the 24th Infantry Division. Though not technically allowed to fight on the front lines, she observed that the line between the front and rear was blurred.

This was due to the sophistication and long ranges of the weaponry that was being used. "Before the ground war started, we were 15 kilometers [9.3 miles] south of the border," she stated. "When the Iraqis lobbed artillery to see where we were, I could feel the vibrations in my chest from the explosions."[2]

At times, Barkalow felt as though support units, such as hers, were at even more risk because they lacked the firepower to properly defend themselves. However, Barkalow said of her time in the Gulf, "We [the men and women of the Army] really pulled together in conditions that were worse than horrible."[3] The decorations Barkalow has received include the Meritorious Service Medal and the National Defense Service Medal.

The first women to enroll at the United States Military Academy, also known as West Point, were admitted in 1976. Those women were members of the class of 1980, pictured here in their first year.

The United States Military Academy

The United States Military Academy (USMA), also known as Army or West Point, is one of the nation's five service academies. (The others are the Naval Academy in Maryland, the Air Force Academy in Colorado, the Coast Guard Academy in Connecticut, and the Merchant Marine Academy in Kings Point, New York.) Located in West Point, New York, the academy was founded in 1801 at a former Army fort on the Hudson River. As is true of all of the service academies, admission to West Point is highly competitive. Tuition is paid for by the military, but students, known as cadets, are required to serve after graduating, and most graduates begin as second lieutenants in the Army. West Point admitted its first female cadets in 1976.

Defensive Shooting

Phoebe Ann Jeter was born on February 21, 1964, in Chester, South Carolina. Jeter, who, during the Gulf War, became the first woman to shoot down Scud missiles, had decided to join the army "for some adventure."[4] In her three years in the Army before going to war, Jeter had practiced destroying surface-to-surface missiles for countless hours. The Persian Gulf War, however, presented her with the opportunity to put her training into action.

During the war, Jeter was in charge of a Patriot missile control team in Riyadh, Saudi Arabia. Her all-male platoon had the task of identifying incoming Scuds, calculating their speed and locations, and then shooting them down with Patriot missiles, US antimissile missiles. "I was in charge of the van that is the engagement control center—where we fire [the Patriot missiles] from. I was the commander inside the van. I was in charge of everything that happened inside that van. It was my responsibility,"[5] Jeter recalled.

Jeter's most memorable experience from the Gulf War came on January 21, 1990. As a Scud alert sounded, Jeter learned that Scuds were headed toward the base in which she worked. Through her gas mask, she shouted commands to her tactical control assistant, ordering the launch of thirteen Patriot missiles in all. When it was all over, the Patriots that Jeter had fired had destroyed two Scuds. For her competence and level-headedness under fire, Jeter became the first woman to receive the Army Commendation Medal in the Gulf. Other decorations that Jeter received include the Army Achievement Medal, the National Defense Service Medal, the Southwest Asia Service Medal, the Army Service Ribbon, and the Army Overseas Service Ribbon.

Treating the Wounded

Stacy Jalowitz-Welter was born on July 25, 1971, in Hayward, Wisconsin. She was the youngest of three girls born to Jim and Sandy Jalowitz. She attended Hayward High School, where she participated in sports such as softball, volleyball, and basketball. Shortly before graduating from high school, Jalowitz-Welter enlisted in the Army National Guard, following in the footsteps of her older sister, Sue, who had joined in 1986.

After graduating high school in 1989, she attended basic training in Fort Jackson, South Carolina, and then advanced individual training in Fort Sam, Texas. She then returned to Wisconsin, where she began classes at the University of Wisconsin–Eau Claire, in the fall of 1990.

A Patriot missile is launched in 1990 at a test range in New Mexico. The Patriot missile is a surface-to-air missile, meaning it is launched at aircraft or other missiles from the ground.

It was during her freshman year at the University of Wisconsin that Jalowitz-Welter's unit, including her sister, was activated. She and her sister left for Saudi Arabia on January 11, 1991, and arrived there two days later.

While in the Gulf, Jalowitz-Welter served as a pharmacy technician in the Thirteenth Evacuation Hospital. Her job included tending to casualties and guarding Iraqi soldiers who had been taken as prisoners. Initially, Jalowitz-Welter lived with her sister on the US air base in Dhahran in an apartment that overlooked the Persian Gulf. Later, her unit transferred to a desert location, just miles south of the Iraqi border. Here, Jalowitz-Welter's unit set up a four-hundred-bed hospital that was used to treat wounded soldiers.

While continuing to do her job, Jalowitz-Welter experienced frequent sandstorms and terrifying Scud alerts, which took place at all hours of the day. After having served for three and a half months in Saudi Arabia, Jalowitz-Welter, along with her unit, flew back to the United States on April 26, 1991. Upon her return home, Jalowitz-Welter returned to the University of Wisconsin–Eau Claire, in order to complete her education. She graduated in 1995 with a bachelor of arts degree in accounting and business administration.

Looking to the Sky

Predicting sandstorms and generally monitoring the weather also proved incredibly important, especially when supporting combat units in unfamiliar territory. During the Persian Gulf War, Barbara Bates served as a meteorologist. Bates was part of a forward-based self-propelled howitzer artillery unit of the 24th Infantry Division (Mechanized). She was the only female in the unit, serving with more than seven hundred artillerymen. As a meteorologist, Bates provided readouts on the local temperature, winds, and other conditions. Though she had a noncombat specialty, the information that Bates obtained was vital to the combat unit that she supported.

Weather was a major concern during Operation Desert Shield and Operation Desert Storm. Rain, clouds, and sandstorms can determine the success or failure of a military operation. Even the most well-equipped army is subject to the limits that terrain, climate, and weather place on it. Therefore, it is very important that meteorologists, such as Bates, study the weather during wartime.

Most of the rainfall in the Gulf region occurs during the months of November and April. The winter months are from December through March. The early-winter months are characterized by fog, rain, and clouds, the cloudier months being December and January. Such rainy and cloudy weather is not conducive to bombing raids or reconnaissance missions. Therefore, it is important that such missions are planned around weather information, such as that provided by Bates during the Gulf War.

Heavy winds, which can cause large sandstorms, are typical in the months of January and February. This season is called the Shammal, which means "north" and describes the winds responsible for the storms. Sandstorms interfere with laser-guided weapons and can potentially clog engines and wear down helicopter blades. The Shammal is also characterized by heavy fog that can make aircraft flight difficult. US and coalition forces experienced sandstorms while in the Gulf. However, when the storms were predicted by meteorologists such as Bates, the military was able to plan around them.

US Marines gather as a unit as a dust storm blows through their camp in Saudi Arabia on December 27, 1990, during Operation Desert Shield.

Between the months of February and April, high winds averaging 35 to 45 miles per hour (56 to 72 kilometers per hour) stir up sandstorms. This is followed by the haboob, a Bedouin word meaning "the worst possible combination of things," so named because of the fast-moving thunderstorms that move along within the sandstorms. Weather like this keeps military radar equipment—which is used to determine the position, size, and velocity of distant objects—from working properly. With the information that Bates provided during the Persian Gulf War, troops were able to make decisions that made the difference between wasted ammunition and good shots.

Supply and Demand

Ora Jane "O. J." Williams stumbled upon the military when, while attending a movie with a friend, she ran into an Army recruiter who was handing out literature. Williams, who at the time was teaching high school home economics and science in Natchez, Mississippi, was looking for a change in career and thought the Army looked interesting. Eight months later, in 1972, Williams began her career with the Army and became a lieutenant by direct commission. Prior to the Persian Gulf War, Williams worked as a protocol officer, an administrative supply officer, a field service company commander, and a logistician. She also served overseas in Germany and South Korea, and attended the Command and General Staff College in Fort Leavenworth, Kansas.

Forty-nine-year-old Williams arrived in Saudi Arabia for Operation Desert Shield in mid-August 1990, having left behind a twelve-year-old adopted son. At the time of her deployment, Williams was a lieutenant colonel with eighteen years of Army service under her belt. During

Soldiers stationed in Kuwait unload supplies from a resupply vehicle. These supplies included ammunition, uniform kits, food, and other necessary items to keep the camp running.

the war, she served as commanding officer of the Second Material Management Center, a battalion-size logistics management unit. Her unit was responsible for the computerized requisition of supplies for the 24th Infantry Division (Mechanized), the 101st Airborne Division, and the 82nd Airborne Division.

Each day, they handled tens of thousands of requests from these combat divisions for important items such as repair parts, clothing, ammo, food, and other supplies. These items were then obtained from either Saudi Arabia or the United States. Though she did not directly engage in combat during the Persian Gulf War, the service that Williams provided as a logistician was vital. Without her, troops would not have had the supplies that they needed in order to carry out their jobs.

Bringing Supplies to the Troops

Cynthia Mosley, a 1984 summa cum laude graduate of Alabama Agricultural and Mechanical University, spent seven months in the Gulf region during Operation Desert Shield/Storm. She served as the commander of Alpha Company, the 24th Support Battalion (Forward), 24th Infantry Division (Mechanized). This battalion was deployed farther forward than any other American supply battalion in Saudi Arabia. Of the four hundred troops in this battalion, nearly a quarter were women.

Mosley's hundred-person unit supplied tank crews and infantry with everything from medicine and food to fuel, ammunition, and spare parts. Mosley's company even had to refuel the forward brigades when all of them ran out of fuel. Without that precious fuel, these brigades would have been stranded, unable to perform their duties. "We were supporting not only the brigade we were assigned," she recalled, "but everybody forward during that particular time in the war."[6] Mosley's unit drove into Iraq just six hours after the fighting, and the memories of the horrific sights she saw would continue to haunt her. However, with resolve she stated, "You just learn to live with it and continue on."[7] For her efforts in the Gulf War, Mosley received the Bronze Star for meritorious service in combat.

Fueling Up

Gianna Nenna Church, nicknamed Gee Gee, was born on March 12, 1960, in Tucson, Arizona. Church joined the Air Force in 1978 and served for five years. After taking a four-year break from the military, she then joined the Army in 1987. During the Persian Gulf War, Church served as a petroleum supply specialist in Saudi Arabia. Units that

Gianna Church received many honors during her military career, including the Southwest Asia Service Medal, pictured here. This award was specifically created to honor those who served in the Gulf War.

were scattered across the desert relied on her, and the convoys of fuel trucks that she drove with, to supply them with fuel. This meant that Church had to travel day and night, getting little or no sleep.

The terrain that the fuel trucks had to travel upon to get to those who needed fuel often presented the drivers with difficulty. To do her job, Church had to drive over rocky land covered with boulders, hills, and sand.

On one occasion, while traveling across some particularly difficult terrain, Church and several other soldiers found themselves stuck in the desert with two flat tires. While stranded in the sand, they were fired upon by Iraqi tanks, small arms, and M203 grenade launchers. One of Church's companions, as well as her truck, was hit. As Church and her companions ran up a hill, they were suddenly blown to the ground. Church was able to escape with her life, but it is an experience that she will never forget.

Church has received many decorations throughout her military career, including the National Defense Service Medal, the Southwest Asia Service Medal, the Army Commendation Medal, and the Army Achievement Medal.

Imprisoned in a War Zone

Historically, prisoners taken during battle were often either executed or enslaved, but in the mid-1600s, policies were introduced to allow captives from both sides to return to their homelands after a peace treaty was signed between the two warring parties on either side of the Thirty Years' War. In the late eighteenth century, combatants on both sides of the Revolutionary War and Napoleonic Wars in Europe created systems for exchanging prisoners even while the war was going on.

Over the past two centuries, international committees have been held about the treatment of prisoners of war (POWs). The most significant of these are the 1907 Hague Convention and the 1929 and 1949 Geneva Conventions. These meetings set forth certain rules of war and treatment of captured enemy combatants, including the prohibition on torturing prisoners. Prisoners are also meant to be granted certain rights. But not all countries adhere to these rules.

During the Persian Gulf War, two female United States military personnel were taken as POWs. They were the first American female POWs since World War II, when eighty-eight women were held prisoner in Germany, Japan, and the Philippines. Both were serving in the Army but were captured under different circumstances. One was taken when her truck became stuck in the desert, and the other after the helicopter in which she was flying was shot down.

Before it was confirmed that women had been taken as prisoners, experts began speculating about how female POWs would be treated. While some believed that any woman held prisoner would be subjected to unspeakable horrors, others believed that women captured in this war would be treated humanely, in light of Islamic law, which states that killing a woman is a serious crime. Both women stated that their captors had essentially treated them well. However, although both women initially claimed that they had not been sexually assaulted, one of the women later revealed that she had been.

A Thirst for Adventure

Melissa Coleman (formerly Rathbun-Nealy), the only child of Leo and Joan Rathbun, grew up in Grand Rapids, Michigan. Coleman attended Creston High School, where one out of ten students joined the junior ROTC program. The ROTC was so popular at the school that a firing range and special classrooms were built in order to accommodate the program. Here, Coleman learned to march, read maps, and shoot a rifle. Coleman graduated from high school in 1988 and joined the Army shortly thereafter. She was seeking adventure and also figured that the Army would be a good way to help her earn money for college.

Following her enlistment in the Army, Coleman was stationed at Fort Bliss, Texas. As a member of the 233rd Transportation Company, she was trained to drive a heavy equipment transporter, a large truck used to transport tanks and other heavy equipment. Coleman served in the Army for two and a half years before she was deployed for Operation Desert Shield.

When Coleman was sent to Saudi Arabia in October 1990, she made it clear that she did not want to be left out of the action. According to Coleman's father, "She told her supervisor that she didn't want to be stuck behind a desk. She wanted to do what she was trained to do."[1]

During the war, Coleman was definitely doing what she was trained to do as she hauled tanks to the front lines. She was also doing what she was trained to do on January 20, 1991, when she was captured by Iraqi soldiers while carrying supplies to the front lines near the border of Kuwait.

On that date, more than three weeks before the hundred-hour ground war began, Coleman was driving in a two-truck convoy when it made a wrong turn. The group ended up accidentally crossing the border from Saudi Arabia into Kuwait, the country being invaded by Saddam Hussein's Iraqi troops. The two trucks found themselves surrounded by Iraqi tanks, armored patrol vehicles, and troops that were moving into the city of Khafji, Saudi Arabia. The trucks were fired upon, but Coleman was unable to escape when her vehicle stalled. "All of the sudden, we hear gunfire, and I just jumped on the floor," Coleman recalled.[2] Both Coleman and her passenger, David Lockett, were injured. She had suffered a shot to the arm, and Lockett had taken several bullets to the chest. They were soon surrounded by ten to fifteen armed Iraqi soldiers and taken prisoner.

The Capture

Coleman and Lockett were then taken to Basra, a military command center and a key port city located just north of Kuwait, and then to a prison in Baghdad, where they received medical treatment. On January 20, the Iraqis stated that allied POWs would be used as human shields against American air attacks on their military sites. This meant that the Iraqi military would move allied POWs to locations that were likely to be bombed by coalition forces in order to deter them from making such attacks. In his despair, Coleman's father wrote a letter to Saddam Hussein, pleading for his daughter's release.

On March 3, 1991, Coleman and Lockett were released, along with four other American POWs, as part of the first prisoner exchange. Soon after her release, Coleman stated that she had been treated well by Iraqi soldiers. Though some prisoners had reported being beaten, starved, and held in solitary confinement,

Sergeant Kara Aguirre of the Ninety-Sixth Transportation Company secures a tank to a heavy equipment transporter like those Melissa Coleman was trained to drive.

Melissa Coleman and her mother (*center*) embrace after Coleman's arrival back in the United States in March 1991. Coleman was released along with several other POWs.

Coleman said that she had been fed three meals a day, had had access to the prison's courtyard, and had been allowed to walk freely down the hall from her cell to a bathroom. "I was just alone, I was by myself, and I had to rely on myself and my mind,"[3] Coleman recalled. Coleman passed the time by singing, talking to herself, and recalling childhood memories.

After her release, Coleman returned to her post in El Paso, Texas, and married Michael Coleman, a fellow Gulf War veteran who had proposed to her before the war. In 1993, Coleman left the military and moved to San Antonio, Texas, where she now lives. The first US servicewoman imprisoned by enemies since World War II, Coleman was awarded the Purple Heart, the National Defense Service Medal, and the Prisoner of War Medal.

During the Persian Gulf War, the US-led coalition forces held more than eighty thousand Iraqis as prisoners of war, all of whom were allegedly treated in accordance with the 1949 Geneva Convention. In later conflicts, however, human rights violations were discovered on the American side.

Representatives from the various countries involved in the Geneva Convention prepare to sign the 1949 agreement.

Humane Treatment

The Geneva Convention is the name for a series of international summits during which various nations drafted agreements governing wartime conduct. The most commonly referenced agreement is the Humanitarian Law of Armed Conflicts, which provides for the humane wartime treatment of medics, civilians, and prisoners. The original Geneva Convention documents were drafted in 1864, but they were significantly updated after the Geneva Convention of 1949 in response to the atrocities of World War II, when millions of prisoners were killed or died from poor treatment while in the hands of the enemy. The 1949 convention states that POWs must be treated humanely and provided with adequate food, shelter, and medical care. They cannot be tortured or forced to reveal information. Not all countries (including the United States) have adhered to these rules all the time, but these laws, at least in theory, ensure that POWs stay relatively safe and sound despite their situation.

The most well-known example of this is the prison at Abu Ghraib. This was where Iraqi POWs taken during the Iraq War beginning in 2003 are known to have been abused and tortured by American soldiers.

An Unexpected Enlistment

Rhonda Cornum was born in Dayton, Ohio. A self-proclaimed tomboy, Cornum played with frogs and learned how to shoot a gun from her grandfather. Cornum came from a long line of strong women, like her great-grandmother, who had been a pilot in the 1930s. Having completed all the requirements of graduation early, Cornum graduated from high school in 1971, after her junior year. She then attended Wilmington College in Ohio for two years on a full tuition scholarship before transferring to Cornell University in New York. Cornum graduated from Cornell with a bachelor of science degree in microbiology and genetics and then remained at the school, pursuing a doctorate in biochemistry.

The Army was the farthest thing from Cornum's mind when, while presenting research on amino acids at a conference, an Army officer approached her. The lieutenant colonel from the Letterman Army Institute of Research at the Presidio of San Francisco was looking for someone to do amino acid metabolic research. Needing a job, Cornum accepted. In 1978, after earning a PhD in nutrition and biochemistry from Cornell, she signed on with the Army.

At first, Cornum had signed on to be a scientist, not a soldier, but she was soon enthusiastic about being in the military. She earned the esteemed Expert Field Medical Badge by marching 12 miles (19 km) with a 35-pound

(16-kilogram) backpack, and for her work parachuting out of planes she received the Airborne Badge.

In 1982, Cornum decided to go to medical school, and she enrolled in the military's Uniformed Services University in Bethesda, Maryland. While in medical school, Cornum met her future husband, Kory, who convinced her to attend the Army's aviation medicine basic course. Here, Cornum learned how to be a flight surgeon—a doctor who cares for pilots. In 1986, Cornum graduated from medical school in the top third of her class and then went to work at Fort Rucker in Alabama. It was here that Cornum was working when the Persian Gulf War began.

The Doctor's Deployment

Cornum was deployed to Saudi Arabia for Operation Desert Shield in August 1990. She served as a flight surgeon for the Army's 229th Attack Helicopter Battalion. As a flight surgeon, Cornum took care of the medical needs of more than three hundred soldiers. During attack missions, her job was to fly behind the Apache attack helicopters and, if one was shot down, to rescue the pilots before they were captured. On February 27, 1991, the last day of the four-day ground war, Cornum answered an emergency call to retrieve an injured Air Force captain, Bill Andrews, who had been shot down behind enemy lines.

While she and seven other crew members were flying in a Black Hawk search-and-rescue helicopter over a seemingly empty desert, they were suddenly fired upon by antiaircraft guns. Though the Black Hawk gunners fired back furiously, the helicopter's back end was blown off, and they crashed into the sand. Five of the eight crew members died as a result of the crash.

UH-60 Black Hawk helicopters have been in use since 1974 in the United States and are utilized by militaries across the world for everything from search-and-rescue to actual combat.

Thirty-six-year-old Cornum suffered two broken arms, a shattered knee, and a bullet to her right shoulder. Cornum, along with the two other surviving crewmen, was taken captive, becoming one of the war's twenty-three POWs.

Soon after her capture, Cornum felt sure that she would be killed as she and another POW were forced to kneel while rifles were pointed at their heads. She recalled, "One of the guards spoke a few words of English and he seemed to say, 'Kill them! Kill them!'"[4] They were not killed but were, instead, moved around to several locations, where they were interrogated.

Capture and Return Home

The first twenty-four hours of her captivity were probably the worst. Cornum was most angered when one of her captors stole her wedding ring. Then, as she was being transported to Basra in the back of a pickup truck, Cornum was sexually assaulted by an Iraqi soldier. However, other Iraqi soldiers were kind to Cornum. Cornum was helpless, due to her arm injuries. Several soldiers helped her to use the bathroom, respectfully averting their eyes. They also fed her bread, water, and vegetables by hand. Cornum was even offered tea. When she was finally taken to a hospital, doctors X-rayed and cast her arms and removed the bullet from her shoulder. Grateful for having made it to a hospital, Cornum sang to herself and prayed, "Thank you, Lord. Thank you, Lord, for getting me here."[5] Finally, after eight days of captivity, Cornum was released, along with fifteen other American POWs, on March 6, 1991.

Following the Persian Gulf War, Cornum was made a colonel, and in the mid-1990s, she commanded an Army

Cornum (*right*) leans against an unidentified woman at a ceremony on March 10, 1991, where a number of Gulf War POWs were honored.

medical unit in Tuzla during the US operation in Bosnia. In 1992, Cornum wrote a book, entitled *She Went to War: The Rhonda Cornum Story*, in which she tells the story of her life and her time spent as a POW.

For her service during the Persian Gulf War, Cornum received the Purple Heart, the Prisoner of War Medal, and the National Defense Service Medal. Cornum said of the POWs held during the 2003 war in the Gulf, Operation Iraqi Freedom, "They can survive this and come out of it OK. I did … I'm fine today."[6]

The Human Cost

Atotal of 294 Americans died in Operation Desert Storm, and about half of those people (149) were considered to have been killed in action, meaning their deaths are directly attributed to enemy combatants rather than to accidents or other injury. Although women serving during the Gulf War were not allowed to serve in combat units like Navy destroyers and Army infantry, they were closer to the front lines than women had ever been allowed in the past. Despite the fact that they were in support positions, women in the military during the Gulf War were often in great danger because of weapons innovations and enemy tactics. Of those who died during Operation Desert Storm, fourteen were women, and five of those fourteen were considered to have been killed in action. One of these women, Marie Rossi-Cayton was killed in a helicopter crash, three others died in a Scud missile attack, and one was killed when a mine exploded.

The Missile Attack: Beverly Sue Clark and Christine Mayes

Beverly Sue Clark was born on May 21, 1967. Clark enlisted in the Army following her graduation from high school in Armagh, Pennsylvania. She attended basic training at Fort Dix, New Jersey, and advanced individual training at Fort Lee, Virginia, as a material storage and handling specialist. Later, Clark went to the 2703 Reserve

Forces School in Pittsburgh, where she was trained as a water purification specialist. Following an assignment with the 1,004th General Supply Company, Clark was then assigned to the Fourteenth Quartermaster Detachment, a water purification unit.

During Operation Desert Shield, the Fourteenth Quartermaster Detachment was one of twenty-two units from the Ninety-Ninth Army Reserve Command to be activated. The unit underwent intense training, at Fort Lee, Virginia, in preparation for deployment to Saudi Arabia. For thirty days, Clark's detachment trained for eighteen hours a day on the reverse osmosis water purification unit (ROWPU), a water purification system. This system was used to produce clean water from undrinkable sources.

Clark's unit arrived in Dhahran, Saudi Arabia, on February 19, 1991. Just five days later, on February 25, 1991, Clark was killed during a Scud missile attack. A Scud missile hit Clark's barracks, a converted warehouse,

Scud missiles, like the one pictured here in 1991, were originally developed by the Soviet Union during the Cold War. The Iraqi military fired many Scud missiles during the Gulf War.

while many of the soldiers were eating dinner, sleeping, and relaxing. In this Scud attack, twenty-eight soldiers lost their lives and ninety-nine others were wounded.

In honor of Clark, an Indiana University of Pennsylvania scholarship was established for the children of the veterans of the Persian Gulf War. Clark received many decorations during her military career, including the National Defense Service Medal, the Southwest Asia Service Medal, the Army Service Ribbon, and the Kuwait Liberation Medal. Clark was also awarded the Purple Heart for having sacrificed her life.

Christine Mayes was killed by the same missile attack that killed Clark. Born in 1968 in Rochester Mills, Pennsylvania, Mayes enlisted in the United States Army after she graduated from high school in 1987. She attended both basic and advanced individual training as a food service specialist at Fort Jackson, South Carolina. Of her three years of active duty, Mayes served two and a half years with the 586th Maintenance Company in Germany. In 1990, Mayes was released from active duty. She then enlisted in the Army Reserve, where she was assigned to the Fourteenth Quartermaster Detachment in Greensburg, Pennsylvania.

When Operation Desert Shield began in 1990, Mayes's unit was one of the twenty-two units activated from the Ninety-Ninth US Reserve Command, the parent unit of the Fourteenth. In the Gulf, her unit served to purify, store, distribute, and issue drinkable water to the ground troops around her. Mayes performed her duty for five days before she was killed in action. The attack took place just hours before orders that told enemy troops to withdraw were announced over Iraqi radio. Mayes, who had gotten engaged just one day before she left for the Persian Gulf, was twenty-two when she died. Mayes received the Army Reserve Component Achievement Medal, the National Defense Service Medal, the Southwest Asia Service Medal, the Army Service Ribbon, the Kuwait Liberation Medal (Saudi Arabia), and the Purple Heart.

Cindy M. Beaudoin

Cindy M. Beaudoin was born on July 20, 1971, in Connecticut. During the Persian Gulf War, Beaudoin served in the 142nd Medical Company of the National Guard as a medic. She was killed in action on February 28, 1991, just hours after a cease-fire was declared.

Beaudoin had been providing medical attention to surrendered enemy soldiers at the Iraq-Kuwait border when an explosion killed her platoon commander and wounded

The Purple Heart

One of the best-known military honors, the Purple Heart is awarded to soldiers who are wounded or killed in action (in which case the medal is granted to their family). The precursor to the Purple Heart, the Badge of Military Merit, was established by George Washington while he was commander of the Continental Army. A heart made of purple fabric, the Badge of Military Merit was awarded to three soldiers by Washington himself, and to other Revolutionary War heroes by his subordinates. In 1932, on the two-hundredth anniversary of Washington's birth, the Purple Heart was reestablished. The first woman to receive the medal was Lieutenant Annie G. Fox, who was wounded during the Japanese attack on Pearl Harbor on December 7, 1941.

several other members of her platoon. She quickly readied herself to fight, but a second explosion mortally wounded her. In a letter that she had written for her parents to open in the event of her death, Beaudoin asked them not to mourn for her. She asked for them, instead, to mourn for all of the men and women who had given their lives so that others could live freely. For her sacrifice, Beaudoin was awarded the Purple Heart.

Marie Rossi-Cayton

Major Marie Therese Rossi-Cayton, a native of Oradell, New Jersey, was born on January 3, 1959. Rossi-Cayton graduated from River Dell Regional High School and entered Dickinson College in Pennsylvania in the autumn of 1976. In 1980, she graduated with a psychology degree from Dickinson College, where she was an ROTC cadet. During the Persian Gulf War, Rossi-Cayton was the commanding officer of Company B, Second Battalion, 159th Aviation Regiment, Eighteenth Aviation Brigade.

She piloted a CH-47D Chinook cargo helicopter, in which she carried supplies to the troops in the combat zone. One-hundred sixty-three CH-47Ds took part in Operations Desert Shield and Desert Storm. In addition to their use in the transportation of troops, artillery, supplies, and equipment to the battlefield, these aircraft were also used for medical evacuation, parachute drops, search and rescue, heavy construction, and firefighting.

Rossi-Cayton's unit was among the first American units to cross into Iraq when the ground war of Operation Desert Storm began. Even though female helicopter pilots had taken part in the 1989 invasion of Panama for Operation Just Cause, this marked the first time that they had crossed a front line. As the 82nd and 101st Airborne Divisions advanced into enemy-held territory, Rossi-Cayton's unit supplied them with needed fuel and ammunition. In an interview conducted by CNN the day before the ground phase of Operation Desert Storm began, Rossi-Cayton showed her willingness for battle when she stated, "This is the moment that anybody trains for, so I feel ready for the challenge."[1]

Rossi-Cayton died on the night of March 1, 1991, the day after the cease-fire had come into effect. She was killed in a helicopter crash near her base in northern Saudi Arabia as she was returning from a supply mission. Rossi-Cayton had been flying in bad weather when her helicopter hit an unlit microwave tower. Along with Rossi-Cayton, three other members of her crew were killed in the crash. The US Army honored her sacrifice in 1992 by naming a small-arms development and testing facility at the Picatinny Arsenal in Dover, New Jersey, the Marie T. Rossi-Cayton Building Armament Technology Facility. In that same year, she was inducted into the Army Aviation Hall of Fame. Rossi-Cayton, who was laid to rest in Arlington Cemetery, was the only female casualty of the Gulf War who was honored in that way. Her gravestone reads, "First Female Combat Commander to Fly into Battle."

The Memorial in Arlington

The Women in Military Service for America Memorial is a living memorial that honors all of the military women who have served, are serving, and will serve on behalf of the United States of America. It is located at the entrance to Arlington National Cemetery in Arlington, Virginia, just south of Washington, DC. On November 6, 1986,

President Ronald Reagan signed legislation authorizing the building of the women's memorial. A retired Air Force brigadier, Wilma Vaught, then spearheaded a campaign that raised more than $20 million to fund its construction. Ground was broken for the memorial in 1995, and it was finally dedicated on October 18, 1997.

Helicopters are highly useful in military situations because of their maneuverability and their ability to land anywhere, but they're also highly dangerous vehicles, both for pilots and those on the ground.

Visitors to the memorial can view the fourteen exhibit areas that display the artifacts, photographs, and writings that were donated by servicewomen and their relatives. Quotes from military servicewomen, etched on a glass arch on the upper terrace of the memorial, represent a sort of journal compiled of women's voices. There are also film presentations, shown in a 196-seat theater, that portray the roles that women have played throughout America's military history. The Hall of Honor recognizes those women who have made extraordinary sacrifices, such as those who were taken prisoner of war and those who died in service. A computerized registry at the memorial is updated regularly and contains hundreds of thousands of personal biographies of some of the two million women who have served from the American Revolution to the present day.

Women in the Military Since Desert Storm

The years following the Persian Gulf War saw changes in the policies and laws governing the roles that women were allowed to play in the military. The women who participated in Operation Desert Shield and Operation Desert Storm did more than just help to liberate Kuwait. Their performances opened up many new roles, and thus thousands of positions, to women in the military. Shortly after the war's end in 1991, Congress repealed the law that restricted women from flying in combat aircraft. This meant that Air Force and Navy women would now be able to pilot fighter and bomber planes. Then, in 1993, the ban on women serving on combat ships was lifted. Navy women were now able to serve on vessels like destroyers, aircraft carriers, and frigates. They were still not allowed to serve on submraines, though that ban was lifted in 2010. Meanwhile, in 1994, Congress set policies allowing women to take part in combat support near the battlefields.

In later conflicts in the Middle East, women comprised an even larger percentage of the armed forces than they did during the Gulf War. Operation Iraqi Freedom, which we

The Women in Military Service for America Memorial is located at an entrance to Arlington National Cemetery near Washington, DC.

now know as the Iraq War, began on March 20, 2003, after Saddam Hussein failed to live up to the agreements of his 1991 surrender. In this war, Army and Marine women came closer to the front lines than ever before. Though women were not allowed to serve directly in ground combat, Air Force and Navy women flew in combat aircraft, and women

First Lieutenant Shaye Lynne Haver (*left*) and Captain Kristen Griest (*right*) show off the new ranger tabs on their uniforms after graduating from the US Army Ranger School on August 21, 2015.

were aboard almost all Navy vessels. Navy women like Heather O'Donnell, Jenn Stillings, and Shannon Callahan flew combat missions as electronic countermeasures officers, working to jam enemy radar and communications signals. As in the first Persian Gulf War, women were also killed and taken as prisoners of war. In one such case, on March 23, 2003, three female Army soldiers were among a dozen who were ambushed when their convoy took a wrong turn in the desert. One of these women died, and the other two, who were taken prisoner, were later rescued.

In January 2013, the policy against women being allowed in combat positions in the United States military was lifted, and in 2016, women were officially allowed to apply for any combat position in the military. In the 2010s, women also began to join certain historically male special operations units: in August 2015, Shaye Lynne Haver and Kristen Griest became the first women to graduate from the US Army Ranger School. In July 2017, the first woman to attempt Navy SEAL training entered the program, but as of 2019 none have graduated to the unit.

A quotation from Rhonda Cornum, former Desert Storm POW, is etched in a glass panel of the Women in Military Service for America Memorial in Arlington, Virginia: "The qualities that are most important in all military jobs—things like integrity, moral courage, and determination—have nothing to do with gender." The courageous women who have served in the military in the past and those who continue to take on the same challenges and roles as men throughout the military absolutely prove this idea.

Chronology

1990 **August 2** Iraq invades Kuwait. President George H. W. Bush orders trade with Iraq to stop.

August 7 Operation Desert Shield begins as the first fighter planes arrive in Saudi Arabia.

August 9 Iraq closes all land borders.

August 22 President Bush calls up reserve troops to active duty.

September 14 The United Kingdom and France deploy troops to the Gulf region.

November 8 The United States sends nearly one hundred thousand more troops to support the forces already in the region.

November 22 President Bush visits US troops for Thanksgiving Day.

November 29 The United Nations authorizes the use of force if Iraq does not leave Kuwait by January 15, 1991. President Bush invites Iraq's foreign minister to meet in Washington, DC.

1991 **January 15** The deadline for Iraq to withdraw from Kuwait passes.

January 17 The air war phase of Operation Desert Storm begins.

January 22 Iraqi soldiers begin to burn the oil fields of Kuwait.

January 25 Iraq dumps millions of gallons of crude oil into the sea.

February 1 Iraq is driven out of Saudi Arabia.

February 23 Iraqis set fire to approximately seven hundred oil wells in Kuwait.

February 24 The ground phase of Operation Desert Storm begins, with Army troops and Marines moving into Iraq and Kuwait.

February 25 An Iraqi Scud missile destroys US barracks in Dhahran, Saudi Arabia, killing twenty-eight soldiers.

February 26 Saddam Hussein announces that Iraq will accept the UN resolution and withdraw from Kuwait.

February 27 President Bush orders a cease-fire.

March 3 Iraq accepts all UN peace resolutions and terms of cease-fire. The first American prisoners of war are freed.

November 7 The final oil fires in Kuwait are extinguished.

Chapter Notes

Chapter 1
Women of the Air Force

1. Jewish Virtual Library, "Lisa Stein," 2003, https://www.jewishvirtuallibrary.org/lisa-stein (accessed May 8, 2019).
2. Muhammad Sadiq and John C. McCain, *The Gulf War Aftermath, an Environmental Tragedy* (Boston: Kluwer Academic Publishers, 1993), p. 2.
3. Peter Grier, "A Quarter Century of AWACS," *Air Force Magazine*, March 2002, Vol. 85, No. 3.
4. Stewart M. Powell, "More Voices from the War," *Air Force Magazine*, June 1991, Vol. 74, No. 6.
5. Maj. Gen. Jeanne Holm, *Women in the Military: An Unfinished Revolution* (Novato, CA: Presidio Press, 1992), p. 452.
6. D'Ann Campbell, "Combatting the Gender Gap [Part 1 of 3]," *Contemporary Women's Issues Database* (Farmington Hills, MI: 1992), pp.13–23.
7. Guy Gugliotta, "Scuds Put U.S. Women on Front Lines," *Washington Post*, January 28, 1991, p. A1.
8. Gugliotta, p. A1.
9. Holm, p. 444.
10. Holm, p. 444.

Chapter 2
Women of the Navy

1. Brenda Holdener, quoted in Eric Schmitt, "The Military Has a Lot to Learn About Women," *New York Times*, August 2, 1992.
2. Judith Bellafaire, "Contributions of Hispanic Servicewomen," Women in Military Service for America

Memorial, 1997, https://www.womensmemorial.org/hispanic-servicewome (accessed May 8, 2019).

Chapter 3
Women on the Ground with the Army

1. Fred Kaplan, "Women Push Limits on Combat Roles," *Boston Globe,* May 28, 1991.
2. Kaplan, "Women Push Limits on Combat Roles."
3. Ellen Goodman, "Military Myths Meet Reality," *Boston Globe,* April 21, 1991.
4. Laura B. Randolph, "The Untold Story of Black Women in the Gulf War," *Ebony*, September 1991, Vol. 26, No. 11, p. 100.
5. Randolph, p. 100.
6. Randolph, p. 100.
7. Randolph, p. 100.

Chapter 4
Imprisoned in a War Zone

1. Maj. Gen. Jeanne Holm, *Women in the Military: An Unfinished Revolution*, revised edition (Navato, CA: Presidio Press, 1992), p. 457.
2. Michelle Koidin, "Female POW: I Wasn't a Hero," Associated Press, January 16, 2001.
3. Diane Jennings, "U.S. Women Endured Captivity in 1991 War," Knight-Ridder/Tribune News Service, March 24, 2003.
4. Greg Barrett, "Treatment Was Bad, but Got Better for Female POW in First Gulf War," Gannett News Service, March 26, 2003.
5. Rhonda Cornum, *She Went to War: The Rhonda Cornum Story* (Novato, CA: Presidio Press, 1992), p. 123.

6. Barrett, "Treatment Was Bad, but Got Better for Female POW in First Gulf War."

Chapter 5

The Human Cost

1. Joseph F. Sullivan, "Army Pilot's Death Stuns Her New Jersey Neighbors," *New York Times*, March 7, 1991.

Glossary

artillery Large mounted firing weapons.

battle group A naval force composed of a varied number of warships, escorts, and supply vessels.

brigade A military unit made up of a large number of troops.

coalition A group formed for a common purpose and for mutual benefit.

combatant A nation engaged in war with other parties.

commission A rank given to an officer in the military.

deploy To bring military forces into action or to strategically distribute military forces.

destroyer A small warship.

frigate A medium-size warship.

howitzer A cannon.

humane Compassionate or kind.

infantry The part of an army that is trained to fight on foot.

logistician A military person who deals with the replacement and the distribution of material and personnel.

mechanize To equip with armed motor vehicles.

protocol officer An officer who deals with the code of ceremony and etiquette that the military follows.

radar A device used to determine the position, size, and velocity of a distant object.

reconnaissance The exploration of an area that provides military information.

requisition To demand things in order to meet the needs of the military.

Scud Russian-made short-range missile.

United Nations (UN) An international organization that was formed in 1945 and includes most of the countries of the world. It was formed to promote peace, security, and economic development.

Bibliography

Barrett, Greg. "Treatment Was Bad, but Got Better for Female POW in First Gulf War." Gannett News Service, March 26, 2003.

Bellafaire, Judith. "Contributions of Hispanic Servicewomen." Women in Military Service for America Memorial, 1997. Accessed May 8, 2019. https://www.womensmemorial.org/hispanic-servicewomen.

Campbell, D'Ann. "Combatting the Gender Gap [Part 1 of 3]." *Contemporary Women's Issues Database.* Farmington Hills, MI: 1992.

Cornum, Rhonda, and Peter Copeland. *She Went to War: The Rhonda Cornum Story.* Novato, CA: Presidio Press, 1992.

Farrel, John Aloysius. "Female Troops Are Getting Closer to Combat Than Ever in U.S. History." *Boston Globe,* January 28, 1991.

Goodman, Ellen. "Military Myths Meet Reality." *Boston Globe,* April 21, 1991.

Grier, Peter. "A Quarter Century of AWACS." *Air Force Magazine,* March 2002, Vol. 85, No. 3.

Gugliotta, Guy. "A Woman's Place: In Command." *Washington Post,* January 23, 1991, pp. B1, B9.

Gugliotta, Guy. "Scuds Put U.S. Women on Front Line." *Washington Post,* January 28, 1991, pp. A1, A9.

Holm, Maj. Gen. Jeanne. *Women in the Military: An Unfinished Revolution,* revised edition. Novato, CA: Presidio Press, 1992.

Jennings, Diane. "U.S. Women Endured Captivity in 1991 War." *Knight-Ridder/Tribune* News Service, March 24, 2003.

Jewish Virtual Library. "Lisa Stein." 2003. Accessed May 2019. https://www.jewishvirtuallibrary.org/lisa-stein.

Kaplan, Fred. "Women Push Limits on Combat Roles." *Boston Globe*, May 28, 1991.

Koidin, Michelle. "Female POW: I Wasn't a Hero." Associated Press, January 16, 2001.

Myers, Meghann. "Almost 800 Women Are Serving in Previously Closed Army Combat Jobs. This Is How They're Faring." *Army Times*, October 9, 2018. https://www.armytimes.com/news/your-army/2018/10/09/almost-800-women-are-serving-in-previously-closed-army-combat-jobs-this-is-how-theyre-faring/.

Myers, Meghann. "First Female Ranger Grads Open Up About the Aftermath and Joining the Infantry." *Army Times*, March 13, 2018. https://www.armytimes.com/news/your-army/2018/03/13/first-female-ranger-grads-open-up-about-the-aftermath-and-joining-the-infantry.

Nickerson, Colin. "Combat Barrier Blurs for Women on the Front Line." *Boston Globe*, November 13, 1990.

Powell, Stewart M. "More Voices from the War." *Air Force Magazine*, June 1991, Vol. 74, No. 6.

P.O.W. Network. "Bio, Rathbun-Nealy, Melissa." March 9, 1991. Accessed May 2019. http://www.pownetwork.org/gulf/rd035.htm.

Ralston, Jeannie. "Women's Work." *Life*, May 1991, p. 56.

Randolph, Laura B. "The Untold Story of Black Women in the Gulf War." *Ebony*, September 1991, Vol. 26, No. 11, p. 100.

Sadiq, Muhammad, and John C. McCain. *The Gulf War Aftermath, an Environmental Tragedy.* Boston, MA: Kluwer Academic Publishers, 1993.

Schmitt, Eric. "The Military Has a Lot to Learn About Women." *New York Times*, August 2, 1992.

Stambaugh, J. J. "New Face Joins Media 'Troops.'" *Knoxville News/Sentinel*, March 28, 2003, p. A13.

Sullivan, Joseph F. "Army Pilot's Death Stuns Her New Jersey Neighbors." *New York Times*, March 7, 1991, p. B1.

Swick, Andrew, and Emma Moore. "The (Mostly) Good News on Women in Combat." Center for New American Security, April 19, 2018. https://www.cnas.org/publications/reports/an-update-on-the-status-of-women-in-combat.

US Navy Office of Information. "United States Navy Biography, Annette Elise Brown." July 16, 2013. Accessed May 2019. https://www.navy.mil/navydata/bios/bio.asp?bioID=54.

US Navy Office of Information. "United States Navy Biography, Elizabeth M. Morris." July 16, 2013. Accessed May 2019. https://www.navy.mil/navydata/bios/bio.asp?bioID=221.

Voisin, Ailene. "Women at Military Schools." *Atlanta Constitution*, October 15, 1995.

Further Reading

Books

Ahmed, Badeeah Hassan. *A Cave in the Clouds.* Toronto, ON, Canada: Annick Press, 2019.

Rauf, Don. *How George W. Bush Fought the Wars in Iraq and Afghanistan.* New York, NY: Enslow, 2017.

Schmermund, Elizabeth. *The Persian Gulf War and the War in Iraq.* New York, NY: Enslow, 2016.

Simons, Lisa. *Women in Combat: Bringing the Fight to the Front Lines.* North Mankato, MN: Capstone Press, 2017.

Staats, Anne McCallum. *Women Heroes of the US Army: Remarkable Soldiers from the American Revolution to Today.* Chicago, IL: Chicago Review Press, 2019.

Websites

National Women's History Museum
www.womenshistory.org
The website for the National Women's History Museum in Alexandria, Virginia, offers digitized exhibits, articles, and other resources about women throughout American history.

US Army Women's Museum
www.awm.lee.army.mil
The United States Army Women's Museum is located in Fort Lee, Virginia, and its website offers a guide to its exhibits and useful articles about women throughout Army history.

Women in Military Service for America Memorial
www.womensmemorial.org
The Women's Memorial in Washington, DC, has educational resources and articles across its website about women in the military.

Index